The Urbana Free Library

To renew: call 217-367-4057
or go to "*urbanafreelibrary.org*"
and select "Renew/Request Items"

A TRUE BOOK™

Extreme Experiments

ANN O. SQUIRE

Children's Press®
An Imprint of Scholastic Inc.
New York Toronto London Auckland Sydney
Mexico City New Delhi Hong Kong
Danbury, Connecticut

Content Editor
Robert Wolffe, EdD
Professor
Bradley University, Peoria, Illinois

Library of Congress Cataloging-in-Publication Data
Squire, Ann, author.
 Extreme experiments / by Ann O. Squire.
  pages cm. — (A true book)
 Audience: 9–12.
 Audience: Grade 4 to 6.
 Includes bibliographical references and index.
 ISBN 978-0-531-20742-0 (library binding : alk. paper) — ISBN 978-0-531-21553-1 (pbk. : alk. paper)
 1. Science—Experiments—Juvenile literature. I. Title.
 Q182.3.S68 2015
 507.8—dc23   2014005455

All rights reserved. Published in 2015 by Children's Press, an imprint of Scholastic Inc.
Printed in China 62
SCHOLASTIC, CHILDREN'S PRESS, A TRUE BOOK™, and associated logos are trademarks and/or registered trademarks of Scholastic Inc.

1 2 3 4 5 6 7 8 9 10 R 24 23 22 21 20 19 18 17 16 15

Front cover: Reactor core at a nuclear power plant

Back cover: Scientist wearing gas mask, holding a smoking flask

Find the Truth!

Everything you are about to read is true *except* for one of the sentences on this page.

Which one is **TRUE**?

T or F   Smallpox was one of the world's most deadly diseases.

T or F   Experiments proved that a horse named Clever Hans could add, subtract, and spell.

Find the answers in this book.

Contents

1 The Ins and Outs of Experiments

How do scientists design experiments?. 7

2 Testing Animals

How did a "smart" horse fool almost everyone?. . 13

3 Space, Time, and Curing the World

How did a gardener's young son help rid the world of a dangerous disease? 21

THE BIG TRUTH!

Cloning a Sheep

What makes a clone different from other offspring? 28

Dolly was the first successfully cloned sheep.

4

The Bikini Islands

4 Risky Endeavors

Why are the beautiful Bikini Islands
impossible to visit? 31

5 Just Plain Weird

How far will scientists go to help
human patients?........................... 39

True Statistics 44

Resources 45

Important Words 46

Index 47

About the Author 48

A surgeon first described using forehead skin to replace an amputated nose in 500 BCE.

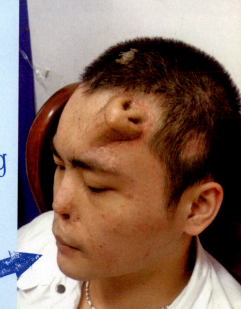

5

A special suit was designed to protect an astronaut during a "walk" in space.

Decades of experiments have made it possible to survive in space.

6

The Ins and Outs of Experiments

An experiment is a way of finding out about the universe. There are so many strange and wonderful things around us. Scientists often design equally strange experiments to learn about them. Think of catching a horse in a lie it didn't know it was telling. Or growing a new ear or nose for a patient to replace one that's been damaged. Some researchers have wiped out dangerous diseases. Others have turned entire islands deadly. No matter their design, experiments change the way we see the world.

Designing an Experiment

An experiment is designed to answer a specific question. Experiments may be very simple or very complex. It depends on what sort of question the experiment is designed to answer. For example, a researcher might ask, "How does wearing a hat affect a person's temperature?" To answer this, the scientist makes a prediction. He or she then designs an experiment that will best test that prediction.

Warmth is just one aspect of hats a scientist can study. A researcher might also study how different hats protect a head from rain or provide shade from the sun.

Testing a Hypothesis

Suppose our scientist predicts that a hat helps a person shiver less. This is called a **hypothesis**. The scientist might take this hypothesis one step further. He or she hypothesizes that the thicker a hat is, the less that person will shiver. To design an appropriate experiment, our scientist must deal with **variables**. Variables are things that could change. There are three kinds of variables: independent, dependent, and constant.

Our researcher learns about how hats affect warmth by giving each subject a different hat to wear.

Variables

The independent variable is a change the scientist controls. He or she tells one person to wear a thick winter hat, another a ball cap, and a third no hat at all. The type of hat each person wears is the independent variable. The amount of shivering each subject experiences is the dependent variable. This variable changes, depending on the independent variable.

Constant variables should not change. The subject's clothing, his or her location, and the weather are examples of what can affect results. Imagine that the first subject wore a long-sleeved shirt and jeans. The other two wore shorts and T-shirts. The first subject shivers the least. Is this because he wore the warmest hat or because of his long sleeves and pants? To trust results, the scientist must keep constant variables the same for all subjects.

Differences in what kind of weather the subjects experience affect an experiment's results.

11

The horse Clever Hans stands with his teacher, Wilhelm von Osten (front).

CHAPTER 2

Testing Animals

Scientists have long asked questions about animals. How much can they learn? How smart are they? A horse in Germany named Clever Hans was famous in the 1800s for his supposed intelligence. Hans could spell, tell time, and solve math problems. When asked a question, Hans tapped the answer with one of his front feet. If asked, "What is 2 plus 3?" Hans tapped his foot five times. People couldn't believe a horse could be so smart.

Hans was trained by a former schoolteacher.

How Does He Do That?

In 1904, a group of researchers concluded that Hans's abilities were real. But this answer was not good enough for a scientist named Oskar Pfungst. Pfungst designed his own experiment. When Hans was kept away from his audience, he answered correctly. When people other than Hans's owner asked the questions, he answered correctly. But when he could not see the questioner or the questioner did not know the answer, Hans failed miserably. What was going on?

Clever Hans's mentor gives Hans a lesson.

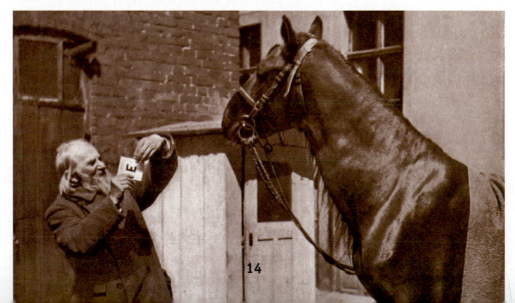

Hans was observant, but not necessarily intelligent.

Subtle Cues

Pfungst found that Hans was responding to almost-invisible cues from his human partner. As Hans tapped an answer, he watched the person closely. When the horse reached the correct number of taps, the person would relax or change expression without realizing it. But Hans noticed this movement. He understood it as a signal to stop tapping. The horse was clueless if the questioner didn't know the answer or was out of sight.

A Mouse with Three Ears

Dr. Charles Vacanti wanted to help people who had injured or lost an ear. He figured out how to make cells from a cow grow into the shape of an ear. But the "ear" needed a blood supply to grow. Dr. Vacanti implanted the cells under a mouse's skin. The mouse's blood nourished the cells. The weird result was a mouse with what looked like a human ear growing out of its back!

Fat Mice

Scientists also study animals to learn more about human problems. Obesity, or being very overweight, is a condition that affects many people. Mice can be obese, too. A type of mouse called "ob/ob" was known for its voracious appetite. Ob/ob mice ate constantly, getting fatter. As adults, ob/ob mice weighed three times as much as normal mice. Scientists wondered why these mice were always hungry, while normal mice knew when to stop eating.

Scientists around the world have been studying different causes of obesity in mice to figure out ways to treat obesity in humans.

Researchers made a small cut down one side of a normal mouse and one side of an ob/ob mouse. Then they sewed the two mice together so the mice shared the same bloodstream. Soon, the ob/ob mouse was losing weight. Researchers found that normal mice have the **hormone** leptin, which controls appetite, in their blood. Obese mice lack this hormone. When the ob/ob mouse shared a bloodstream with the normal mouse, it received the hormone and ate less. Scientists have found that leptin affects humans, too.

Both of these mice are ob/ob mice. The mouse on the right has been given the hormone leptin.

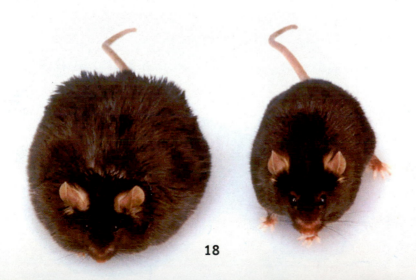

Animal Experiments: Right or Wrong?

The results of animal experiments can be tremendously valuable to humans. But is it appropriate to do these experiments? Some people argue that experimenting on animals is a small price to pay for advances in human health. Others say it is unfair to inflict pain or discomfort on animals for any reason at all. People have been debating these questions for many years. Unfortunately, there are no easy answers. What's your opinion?

An astronaut floats outside the International Space Station.

CHAPTER 3

Space, Time, and Curing the World

Can you imagine spending three months in bed? If so, you might qualify for the National Aeronautics and Space Administration's (NASA) bed rest study. It measures the effects of **microgravity** on the human body. This applies to astronauts spending long periods of time at the International Space Station 230 miles (370 kilometers) above Earth. It also helps experts plan future space missions.

A lab in space lets scientists study how space travel affects the human body.

Living in Bed

Participants spend three months lying down. Their heads rest about 6 inches (15 centimeters) lower than their feet. Eating, sleeping, showering, and using the bathroom are all done in this position. Without exercise, a person's bones and muscles get weaker and fitness level decreases. This is similar to what happens in a weightless environment. Some research subjects do exercises while in bed. Scientists hope these experiments will show how to keep astronauts healthy in space.

A test subject is helped out the door after spending 12 weeks in bed in NASA's bed rest study.

A Year in Bed

If you think three months in bed sounds boring, consider another experiment conducted in the 1980s. The test included 11 subjects in the Soviet Union, which is now Russia and surrounding countries. The volunteers spent 370 days in bed. The purpose of the experiment was the same as NASA's. It turned out that one of the biggest problems the subjects faced was boredom. Nevertheless, only one man quit the experiment before the year was up.

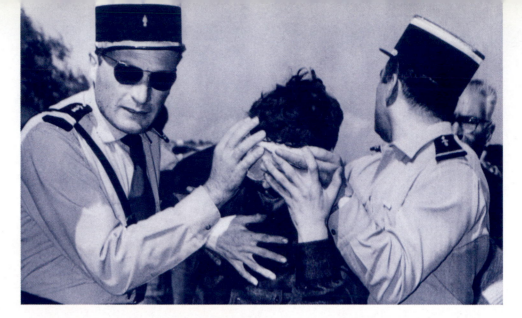

Two police officers help Michel Siffre after his first cave experiment. Siffre had to cover his eyes to protect them from the light after being in the dark cave.

Life Underground

You might volunteer to spend a few months in bed. What about spending that time in a cave? This is what Michel Siffre did. In 1962, Siffre spent two months underground. He wanted to know how living without the sun or a clock would affect his understanding of time. His only access to the outside world was a phone line. He used this to report each time he woke up, ate, and went to sleep.

Internal Time

Despite having no way to tell time, he still slept and woke on a cycle lasting just over 24 hours. He lost track of the days, though. When his team came to get him at the end of the experiment, he thought he still had a month to go. In later experiments, many other subjects developed a roughly 48-hour cycle. They were awake for 36 hours and then slept for 12 to 14 hours.

Siffre took part in a second cave test in 1972. He spent 205 days in a cave in Texas.

The First Smallpox Vaccine

Would you test a **vaccine** for a deadly disease? Some experts estimate that smallpox has killed more people than all other infectious diseases combined. Smallpox causes fever, aches, and blisters that cover the body. Researchers had long looked for ways to prevent or cure smallpox. In the late 1700s, 13-year-old Edward Jenner heard that

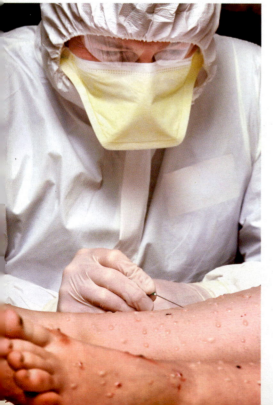

people who caught the mild cowpox **virus** never caught smallpox. As a medical student years later, Jenner hypothesized that exposure to cowpox could prevent smallpox.

Smallpox has affected people of all ages around the world.

Nearly 200 years after Jenner's experiments, the world was officially declared free of smallpox.

A Risky Test

Jenner first tested his prediction in 1796. He chose the eight-year-old son of his gardener as his subject. He infected the boy with cowpox. The boy developed a blister and a fever, but recovered. Then Jenner gave the child the smallpox virus. To everyone's relief, he did not develop the disease. Jenner's experiment led to the creation of a smallpox vaccine. Vaccines have since been developed for many diseases, including polio, measles, and tetanus.

Cloning a Sheep

In 1996, scientists in Scotland made history. They managed to clone a sheep, which they named Dolly. To do this, they used DNA. DNA is the blueprint for how an individual organism develops.

In normal reproduction, an organism gets DNA from both the mother and the father. The parents' DNA combines, mixing characteristics. For example, you may have gotten blue eyes from your father and left-handedness from your mother. You may be similar to both of your parents, but you are not exactly like either of them.

A clone is different. It is an exact copy of another organism. In Dolly's case, DNA was taken from a cell in her mother's body. This was inserted into an egg cell without any DNA from another sheep. Because she developed entirely from her mother's DNA, Dolly was an exact copy of her mother. In fact, she was her mother's identical twin!

Since then, mice, cows, pigs, deer, and other animals have been cloned. But as scientists learn more about the cloning process, there is concern that the technology could one day be applied to humans. Many people are afraid of what this could do to our species. What do you think?

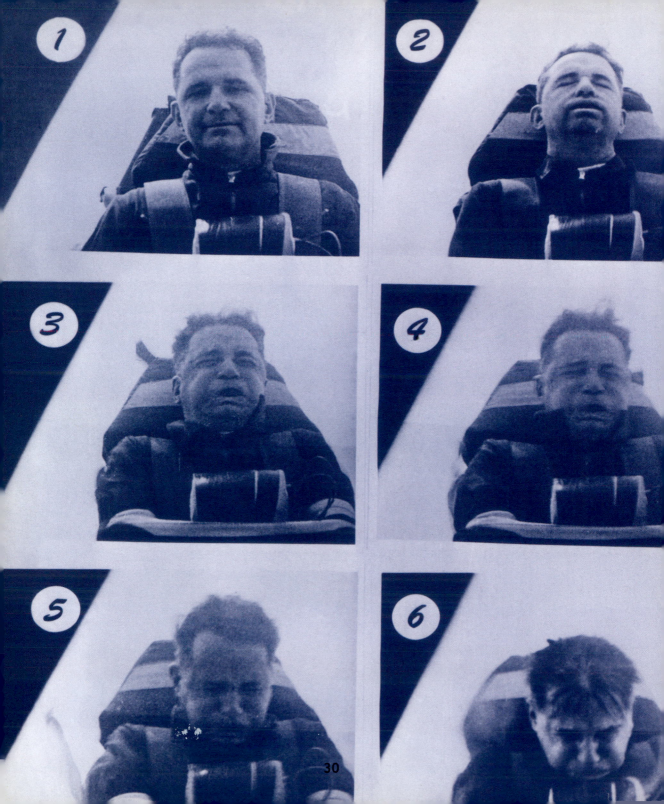

Risky Endeavors

Some experiments can be incredibly dangerous. In the past, researchers at times chose to experiment on themselves instead of putting other subjects at risk. John Paul Stapp, a doctor and U.S. Air Force officer, was one of these researchers. He wanted to know if pilots could safely eject from planes traveling at the speed of sound. To test this, Stapp rode a "rocket sled." The sled reached superfast speeds before slamming to a stop.

During his experiments, Stapp used safety measures such as harnesses.

Experts estimate that seat belts saved almost 63,000 lives in the United States between 2008 and 2012.

The Fastest Man Alive

On December 10, 1954, Stapp set a land speed record. He reached 632 miles (1,017 km) per hour in five seconds.

The accomplishment made him famous. He used his fame to push for better safety harnesses in military aircraft. He also argued for safety belts in cars. Thanks in part to Stapp, President Lyndon Johnson signed the Highway Safety Act in 1966. The law required seat belts in all new cars sold in the United States.

As a result of his high-speed experiments, Stapp suffered many injuries. He had concussions, or serious head injuries. He also suffered cracked ribs, broken bones, and permanent vision problems. He once explained, "I took my risks for information that will always be of benefit." Researchers search for ways to protect their subjects during such dangerous experiments. Experiments today are sometimes limited in the interest of safety.

Technicians make last-minute adjustments to John Stapp and his rocket sled before a test.

Atomic Bomb Tests

One of the most dangerous experiments in human history took place on Bikini Islands. This is a group of beautiful tropical islands in the Pacific Ocean. The U.S. military tested the effects of **atomic weapons** on anchored ships there. Bikini Atoll was chosen because it was very isolated. There were 167 people living on the Bikini Islands at the time. They were moved to another island and told they could return after the tests were completed.

Islanders move their belongings during the evacuation of Bikini Atoll in 1946.

A total of 23 nuclear experiments were conducted at Bikini between 1946 and 1958.

On July 25, 1946, an atom bomb was detonated 90 feet (27 meters) beneath the ocean's surface. It sent a column of water 2,000 feet wide (610 m) into the sky. Many ships anchored for the test were destroyed. On the ocean floor, the blast created a crater more than 200 feet (61 m) deep. But the most serious damage was invisible. The bomb released a cloud of **radioactivity**. It contaminated the lagoon and everything in it.

Bikinians discuss the fate of their islands.

The Bikinian people were eager to return to their islands. However, radioactive contamination from the blasts was longer lasting than anyone had predicted. It was not until the 1970s that Bikinians were allowed to move back home. The United States continued to measure radiation levels. After several years, researchers found that radiation levels in the plants, animals, and well water were still dangerously high. Once again, the residents had to leave their islands.

Bikini Atoll Today

The Bikini atomic tests have been widely criticized as overly dangerous and badly designed. If you visited Bikini Atoll today, you would see blue skies, white sand, sparkling clear water, and palm trees swaying in the breeze. But the soil of this tropical paradise is still contaminated with radioactive material. Plants that grow in the soil and animals that eat the plants all carry that radioactivity. The islands are still too dangerous for people to inhabit.

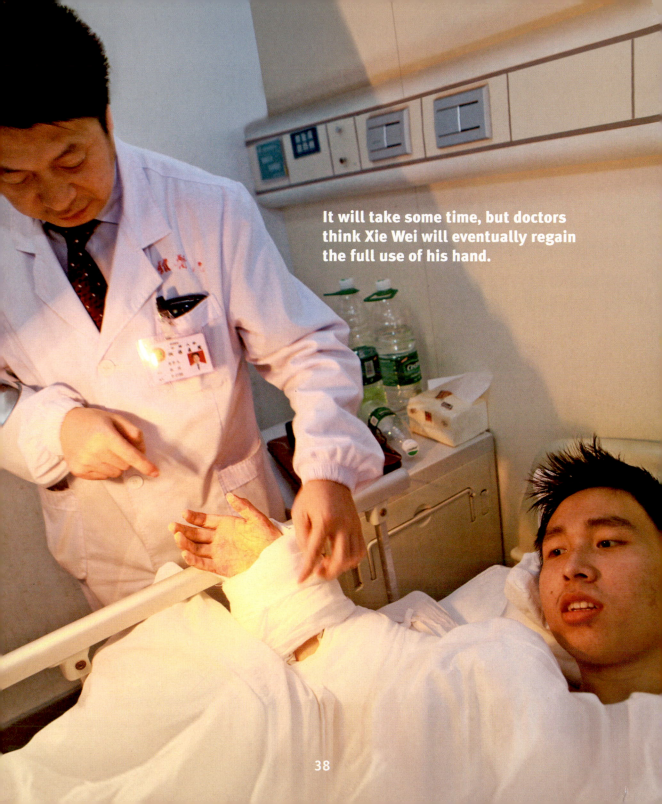

It will take some time, but doctors think Xie Wei will eventually regain the full use of his hand.

Just Plain Weird

Some experiments are so strange that you have to see them to believe them. A Chinese factory worker named Xie Wei was operating a drilling machine when it accidentally cut off his right hand. The quick-thinking worker placed the hand in a bag of ice. He set out to look for a doctor who might be able to reattach it. After visiting several hospitals, he finally found one that could perform the delicate surgery.

Doctors reconnect blood vessels, nerves, muscle, and bone to reattach a severed limb.

A Healthy Hand

However, Xie Wei's arm was badly injured. It needed time to heal before surgeons could reattach his hand. The doctors decided to temporarily attach the hand to Xie Wei's ankle. The ankle's blood supply would keep the hand alive until his arm healed. Xie Wei spent the next month as the only man in the world with a hand sticking out of his leg. Then doctors were able to reattach his hand to his arm.

Timeline of Extreme Experiments

1796
Edward Jenner performs his first vaccination experiment.

1904
A team of researchers declares Clever Hans's abilities to be real.

1946
Researchers perform the first Bikini Atoll atomic test.

A Nose on His Forehead

If you think the last experiment seems weird, consider the case of another Chinese man. He hurt his nose in a traffic accident. Doctors could not repair the nose. They decided to grow a new one—on the man's forehead! Though it looks extreme, the method is similar to other procedures that are used all the time. The doctors first placed expanders under the forehead's skin to create space for the new nose to grow.

1962
Michel Siffre spends two months in a cave.

1996
The world's first successfully cloned sheep, Dolly, is born.

1954
John Paul Stapp sets a land speed record in his rocket sled.

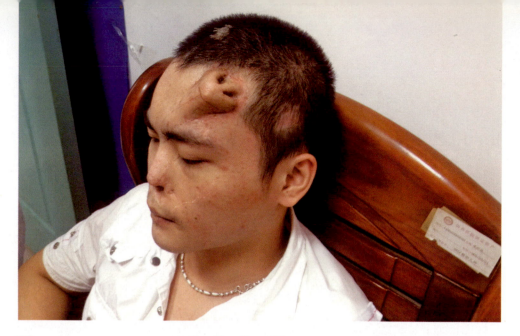

The nose was grown on the forehead because a person's skin at the forehead is similar to the skin on the person's nose.

Next, the man's doctors took cartilage from his ribs to fill in the nose. Cartilage is the tough, flexible tissue that gives a nose its shape. The blood supply in the man's forehead nourishes the new nose as it grows. When the nose is ready, the doctors will move it to the spot currently occupied by the damaged nose. A small scar on the man's forehead will be the only reminder of his strange experience.

An Ear on Her Arm

In a similar case, a woman's cancer treatments badly damaged her ear. Doctors implanted cartilage from her ribs under the skin of her forearm. A new ear grew there for several months, and then was repositioned to the woman's head. She had some fun with the ear's unusual original location. When her children nagged her, she rolled up her sleeve and said, "Tell it to the arm!" Successes like this are what keep doctors and other researchers experimenting. ★

Researchers are always experimenting with new ways to solve problems. What seems strange today may seem perfectly normal years from now!

True Statistics

Number of U.S military and civilian personnel involved in the Bikini atomic experiments: More than 42,000

Number of people killed by smallpox during the 20th century: 300 million

Date of the last known natural case of smallpox: 1977

Estimated number of lives saved each year through the use of seat belts in automobiles: As many as 15,000

Percentage of adults in the United States who are obese: 35.7%

Estimated annual medical cost of obesity in the United States: $147 billion (2008 dollars)

Did you find the truth?

T Smallpox was one of the world's most deadly diseases.

F Experiments proved that a horse named Clever Hans could add, subtract, and spell.

Resources

Books

Marrin, Albert. *Dr. Jenner and the Speckled Monster: The Discovery of the Smallpox Vaccine*. New York: Dutton Juvenile, 2002.

Taylor, Theodore. *The Bomb*. New York: HMH Books for Young Readers, 2007.

Time for Kids Big Book of Science Experiments. New York: Time Home Entertainment Inc., 2011.

Important Words

atomic weapons (uh-TAH-mik WEP-uhnz) — weapons that explode with great force, heat, and bright light; the explosion results from the energy that is released by splitting atoms

clone (KLOHN) — to grow an identical plant or animal from the cells of another plant or animal

hormone (HOR-mone) — a chemical substance made by the body that affects the way the body grows, develops, and functions

hypothesis (hye-PAH-thi-sis) — an idea that could explain how something works but that has to be tested through experiments to be proven right

microgravity (mye-kroh-GRAV-ih-tee) — a condition, especially in space orbit, where the force of gravity is so weak that weightlessness results

radioactivity (ray-dee-oh-ak-TIV-ih-tee) — the harmful particles given off by materials made of atoms whose nuclei break down

vaccine (vak-SEEN) — a substance containing dead, weakened, or living organisms that can be given as a shot or taken by mouth; a vaccine protects a person from the disease caused by the organisms

variables (VAIR-ee-uh-buhlz) — things that are likely to change

virus (VYE-ruhs) — a very tiny organism that can reproduce and grow only when inside living cells

Index

Page numbers in **bold** indicate illustrations

astronauts, **6**, **20**, 21, 22
atomic weapons, 34–36, **35**, 37, 40

bed rest study, 21, **22**, **23**
Bikini Atoll, **34–36**, **35**, **37**, 40

cave study, **24**, **25**, 41
Clever Hans, **12**, 13, **14**, **15**, 40
cloning, 28–**29**, **41**
constant variables, 9, 11
cosmonauts, **23**
cowpox, 26, 27

dependent variables, 9, 10
DNA, 28, 29
Dolly, 28, **29**, **41**

ears, **16**, 43

hands, **38**, 39, 40
hats, **8**, **9**, **10**, **11**
Highway Safety Act (1966), 32
hormones, **18**
horses, **12**, 13, **14**, **15**, 40
hypotheses, 8, 9, 26

independent variables, 9, 10
International Space Station, **20**, 21

Jenner, Edward, 26, **27**, **40**

land speed records, 32, **41**
leptin, **18**

mice, 16, **17–18**, 29
microgravity, 21

National Aeronautics and Space
    Administration (NASA), 21, **22**, 23
noses, 41–**42**

obesity, **17–18**
"ob/ob" mice, **17–18**
Osten, Wilhelm von, **12**, 13, **14**

Pfungst, Oskar, 14, 15
predictions. *See* hypotheses.

questions, 8, 13, 19

radioactivity, 35, 36, 37
"rocket sled" study, **30**, **31**, 32–**33**, **41**

safety, 31, **32**, 33
seat belts, 31, **32**
sheep, 28, **29**, **41**
Siffre, Michel, **24**, **25**, 41
smallpox, **26**, 27
Soviet Union, 23
space exploration, **6**, **20**, 21, 22
speed of sound, 31
Stapp, John Paul, **30**, 31, 32–**33**, **41**
surgery, **38**, 39, 40, 41–**42**, 43

timeline, **40–41**

Vacanti, Charles, 16
vaccines, 26, 27, 40
variables, **9**, 10–**11**
viruses, **26**, 27

Xie Wei, **38**, 39, 40

About the Author

Ann O. Squire is a psychologist and an animal behaviorist. Before becoming a writer, she studied the behavior of rats, tropical fish in the Caribbean, and electric fish from central Africa. Her favorite part of being a writer is the chance to learn as much as she can about all sorts of topics. In addition to the Extreme Science books, Dr. Squire has written about many different animals, from lemmings to leopards and cicadas to cheetahs. She lives in Long Island City, New York.